101 Truths

For You

Truths to Encourage and Guide You Along This Journey of Life

Dedication

This book is dedicated to:
my god-daughter, Saniya Nubia Desilva,
my "adopted brother" Kenneth Moss,
my "little sisters" Ebony and Lacheera Brown,
my "little brother" Deandra Holland,
and my nephew, William McKinley Thomas.
I love you all dearly! As you grow and mature,
may these truths guide and help you along the way.
Remember when you keep God in it, there is no limit!

Table of Contents:

.

 Preface

Why was this book written? This book was written to help navigate you through the journey of life. Dictionary.com defines truth as, "conformity to fact or actuality". As you go through life, you will find that there are many things that you may have believed to be true, but later found out they are not. Reflect on how the untruth (lie) made you feel? Sometimes the truth may be difficult to accept. However, in accepting the truth about yourself, your friends, your family and every other entity in life, you will be able to move on and live a productive life.

Truths are meant to be acknowledged, as they can act as a precaution, providing protection or warning. Some people choose to travel through life shunning and/or hiding the truth, only to have the truth return to haunt them. Identifying the truths in your life will potentially help you to understand your motives and ambitions. In most recovery programs, they teach you that the first step to recovery is to "admit" your problem. Admitting or taking ownership can be difficult; nevertheless, it is necessary for complete recovery. If you are incapable of admitting, you will never be able to accept the truth. Accepting untruths can cause you to live below your potential. Furthermore, untruths can cause you to believe in a false reality, and tend to offer false hopes. Harboring untruths can lead to the destruction of healthy relationships, careers, goals and dreams, potentially creating cycles of hurt and un-forgiveness. '101 Truths for You' serves as a catalyst to generate a change in your thinking.

Moreover, this book offers 101 truths which are believed to be essential to coping with life's events. To the reader, it becomes evident that one cannot accept the truths mentioned without first denying one's self, and realizing that God is the ultimate source and authority in life. Many people suffer with low self-esteem, and this book helps to remind them that they are fearfully and wonderfully made by God. It seeks to identify the definition of true beauty.The book encompasses four compartments: Truths for You; Truths About Your Life; Truths About People (family and friends); and Truths About Life, Love and God's Promises for You. Following each section are scripture guides to further encourage and provoke the reader to thought. I encourage you to compose a truth of your own after you finish reading this book. The truth that you develop will be one that I challenge you to hold onto throughout your life. Let it guide you and remind you that you are never alone.

Also, included are several affirmations and acronyms which were derived to help increase memorization of each truth. In addition to writing a truth for yourself, I encourage you to pass this book along to someone else. That someone else may be an individual struggling with their identity, someone who may think their life is pointless, or someone who may not know Jesus and seeks to develop a relationship with Him. I encourage each of you to stand on His promises and truths in the scriptures. Believe and succeed; remember, with God all things are possible! If you find yourself blessed by the words contained in this book, please take it and bless someone else.

Truths

For You

101 Truths

Truth #1

**Truth is...you are nothing without God!
He is the creator of the universe and mankind;
if you are looking for Him,
He can be accessed through Jesus Christ!**

God is the reason you are everything that you are.
Acknowledging this will teach you humility, which is a
major key to life.

101 Truths

Truth #2

Truth is...you are amazing!

He (God) has equipped you with skills and abilities to do the impossible; all you have to do is believe. You have the ability to do so much; believe in yourself and others will too.

101 Truths

Truth #3

Truth is...you are intelligent.

You cannot accept labels of learning disabilities. Intelligence has nothing to do with how much you know; however, it has everything to do with how you make decisions based on what you know.

Truth is...you are beautiful.

Look in the mirror and repeat this affirmation: "I am who God made me; I am the image of perfection...His perfect creation. I will love ME and accept my faults as they contribute to my originality!"

101 Truths

Truth #5

Truth is...you can do anything that you set your mind to do.

You may be reading this book and saying, "I wish I could write a book." Well, who is stopping you? Do you remember Philippians 4:13 (NIV)? This is one of my favorite verses and I hold on to its promise. With God there is no LIMIT to what you can do!

Raise the B.A.R.

Believe His promises that are written in the Book of Life (the Bible).

Achieve your desires through Him (God).

Receive your blessings and breakthrough.

Truth is...the only restriction in your life is you.

The excuses you make for why something cannot be done are limitations that you put on yourself; therefore, it is a restriction! Remove the chains of fear and doubt that are limiting your movement. Free yourself and LIVE.

101 Truths

Truth #7

Truth is...you can talk yourself out of your blessing.

Have you ever sat and doubted whether or not something was for you? Entertaining such thoughts can cause you to believe that you are NOT good enough to have whatever you desire. I am here to tell you, that sense of doubt is a trick of the enemy (Satan)!

God has a lot in store for you, but how bad do you want it? Are you willing to fight (not physically, but spiritually) for it? If your answer is YES, be prepared to be victorious!

Truth is...you are not perfect, but you are worth it!

No one is perfect; it is our imperfections that make us unique.
However, when you make a mistake, repent and go on your way.
Jesus already paid the price with his death on Calvary;
He died for you and for me.

101 Truths

Truth #9

Truth is...your "neighbor" is everyone who you meet.

We are required to be kind to everyone. We never know when we may be "entertaining angels" (Hebrews 13:2 NIV). A simple smile can help to brighten someone's day. Have you smiled today?

Truth #10

Truth is...your words are powerful.

"Sticks and stones may break your bones", but words actually penetrate the soul. This familiar phrase couldn't be farther from the truth. Words are far more powerful than we think. They stick with you longer than anything you could imagine. So, I encourage you to be mindful of what you say; speak life to someone today!

Truth is...you have to work hard for what you want in life.

Here is a hint for you....if something "good" in your life comes too easily, it may not be the best thing for you, and you may not appreciate it as much. However, hard work usually causes you to appreciate what you have, leaving you with a sense of accomplishment and pride.

Truth is...you should live your dream.

What do you want out of life? There are many who will respond by saying, "Well I want to be like _____ (whomever they admire)." As you go through life, you will realize that aspiring to be like the people you admire may not turn out as effective as you thought. When this occurs, you need to look within yourself, build your own dreams, and begin achieving them.

Truth #13

Truth is...you are unique.

Each person has unique talents and abilities. We all may share similarities, but the truth of the matter is that your differences are what define you. We certainly see this reigning true for multiples, such as twins, triplets, etc. Although many multiples are classified as "identical", there truly are no two people who are exactly alike.

Bottom line is....

EMBRACE YOUR UNIQUENESS!

101 Truths

Truth #14

Truth is...you can be your biggest fan.

Be Confident; confidence says, "Yes, I know I am capable.
I will hold my head up high, for I have nothing to hide."

101 Truths

Truth #15

Truth is...you will face many trials.

If anyone has ever told you that life will be easy, they lied! The truth remains that you will encounter many trials and hardships. However, what matters most is your attitude during these times. Will you give up and lose hope?

101 Truths

Truth #16

Truth is...you're more than likely responsible for some of the trials in your life.

As humans, we have been given the gift of free will; with this gift, we make choices that can sometimes cause us pain and heartache, usually producing trials in our life.Learn to decipher whether a trial is a result of a consequence of wrong actions/decisions. Accept the blame and pray that He (God) will help you through the trial. Lastly, allow God to guide the decisions that you make going forward.

Truth is...we sometimes put too much trust in people.

There are some people who have not learned to censor what they share with others around them. Be mindful of whom you trust and share information. Some people are only there to take information that you've shared, and use it to pass judgment upon you. If you are looking for a friend to constantly be around you, just talk to God! Put your trust solely in Him; He is a perfect being who will NEVER let you down!

101 Truths

Truth #18

Truth is...we sometimes take many things for granted.

Our basic senses, for example, are things we often take for granted. There are people who have many of the necessary functions of the body, yet they are not able to walk, talk, see or hear. It's seemingly the little things that we often take for granted, usually causing us to forget to thank God. Stop for a moment and give thanks for those little things!

Truth is...you are not controlled by your circumstances.

Your circumstances do not define who you are....YOU personally define it. Repeat after me, "I am in control of my circumstances. There are things I may not like or cannot change, but I know that God will make a way. I will be victorious if I keep God in focus."

Truth is...you should stop complaining and start praising!

No one likes to hear people complain, especially if it is a constant occurrence. Before you open your mouth to complain, pause and think…"things could be worse." Take time to reflect on all the good things that are occurring and be content knowing that "this too shall pass".

Truth is...you should never allow someone/something to alter your mood. When you do, you've just given them control over your well-being.

When just the mere thought of a person or a situation can alter your mood, you've in essence given that particular thing or person control over your state of being. Release it through forgiveness and set yourself free. Tell that person or thing, "NO longer shall you restrict and control me; I am free!"

Truth is...you have to channel the positive.

This is not an easy task; nevertheless, it must be done. Positivity will take you far. You can begin to channel positive thinking by ingesting (taking in) positive affirmations and good, positive music; as well as by eliminating negativity and drama from your life.

101 Truths

Truth #23

Truth is...your miracle is on the way.

Remind yourself of this truth every time you are faced with adversity or trials. After every storm comes a rainbow (a ray of hope); the rainbow serves as a reminder that there is "light at the end of the tunnel".

Truth is...your blessing is already here and it is simply YOUR LIFE!

I always say, "Be a blessing to someone, because you are already blessed." Every day you wake up is a blessing. Please recognize this before it is too late!

Truth is...your career should involve something that you love to do.

When you pursue something you love to do, you will give it your all. A career should not be a headache or a bothersome part of your day. If you are unhappy where you are, you need to re-evaluate your purpose there. Rekindle the fire you once had and enjoy the things you love.

Truth is...referring to oneself in derogatory terms gives others the right to do it as well.

I REFUSE to address myself using any derogatory titles. I really find it disturbing when others refer to themselves as such. When you do this, you are giving everyone else permission to address you in that same manner, so please do not be upset when they do!

Truth is...you have the power to control your emotions.

Learning to control your emotions (how you react) amongst people and in situations is a process. However, mastery in this area will make you victorious.

Truth is...you can choose whether to hurt or not to hurt.

You may have endured lots of hardships and trials, but those hurts are a thing of the past. In order to live an effective life, you cannot allow the hurt you feel to hold you back. Choose to push beyond the hurt and pain, and never use your hurt as a crutch. Instead, choose to love; knowing that healing will come. Love yourself until you forget the hurt you endured. Remember, God loves you more than words can express.

Truth is...we sometimes allow negative things to happen.

There are some things in life that we allow to happen because we chose to ignore the warning signs, or we simply become inactive and hope for the best. Learn to listen to that inner voice. If you no longer hear those voices of conscience, pray that God speaks to you again. Do not sit there helpless when you are capable of stopping whatever negative cycles you may be creating.

101 Truths

Truth #30

Truth is...we sometimes ignore the warning signs in our relationships.

The voice of conscience is a guide; certain traits you see in others should not be ignored. Take action and head for the door!

Truth is...your main task in life is to help someone else in need.

I have often sought to find my purpose in life. Although our true purpose is unique, we are all given the same task, which is to focus less on ourselves and help others in need.

101 Truths

Truth #32

Truth is...your passion is your drive.

Examine yourself and identify your passion. What motivates you? What gives you a feeling of gratification? Find this passion, fuel it, and allow your passion to take you to higher heights.

101 Truths

Truth #33

Truth is...we should be mindful of personal appearance and the nonverbal messages we convey.

Dressing provocatively and acting in a demeaning manner only brings shame and embarrassment. We begin to send the wrong message and create a false reality. Be who you are, and not who others want you to be. Create your own style and embrace your individuality.

Truth is...you need to recognize when you are "self medicating".

Oftentimes, people use food, drugs, alcohol, sex, and other vices as a form of medication. Any hurt or traumatic experience has the ability to leave you clinging to this "medication" as a means of coping. Learn to recognize what's your choice of medicating, and seek help in addressing that particular issue. Overuse of "medication" can lead to fatal destruction. I value you. I hope you value yourself too!

101 Truths

Truth #35

Truth is...you each have a story.

Your life events are unique to you; others may be able to relate to what you have been through, but they can never fully relate to YOU. Endure through life's events and live to share your motivating story of triumph.

Truth is...everyone is talking about you...choose what you listen to.

Your life is a like a television set....always on display. People talk about what they see, hear, think, believe or even imagine. There may be some negative things said about you; therefore, you should choose wisely what you listen to. Don't allow people's opinions to cause you hurt and shame.

Truth is...there is a leader in you.

You were born to lead; we each possess leadership abilities and qualities. The type of leader you are is a matter of choice.
Today, decide to channel those positive leadership
abilities, and encourage others
to channel theirs as well.

Truth is...you have to be careful of what you ask of God.

Some may disagree, but I believe the enemy/devil can hear prayers too. Sometimes he can send a false hope or reality, and we think that it is God speaking. Remember, the enemy is a master of disguise; he can deceive us into believing that something is the will of God, when in actuality it isn't. Please be mindful when this occurs. Before you react, think and pray to God.

Truth is...the more you act, the louder you speak.

I often tell people, "I am mute to your mere words. SHOW me, and I will hear what it is you are trying to say." I read body language and interpret what people are trying to say through their actions. Most of the time, their actions and speech do not align with one another. Seek to find balance between the two; people are highly affected by the things you do.

Truth #40

Truth is...your fears can be your road blocks.

Have you ever began a journey and reached a dead end? Those dead ends can represent fears and may seem like there is no way out. Hope represents the rerouting that the "GPS navigation" provides. Release fears and allow alternative hope and change to come into your life.

Truth is...you have to accept responsibility for your actions.

One of the marks of being an adult is learning to fully accept responsibility for your actions. It takes a lot for an individual to admit when they may be wrong, but in the end, admitting our wrong speaks volumes. Remember, no one is perfect, but we are all worth it!

Truth is...you never stop growing.

"They" say after a certain age, your growth ceases. Despite many of you having reached your physical growth limit, you should never stop growing spiritually. This growth occurs when you become engrossed in the "Book of Life" (the Bible). The content of this "Book of Life" contains great truths and promises for us all.

101 Truths

Truth #43

Truth is...there is always something to learn.

It has always been a goal of mine to learn something new every day. It does not matter how minute the information may be, but the mere fact that I seek this goal shows that I appreciate my ability to learn. Nevertheless, it is unfortunate that we often take this ability for granted. Let's pause a moment and give thanks for this ability!

Truth #44

Truth is...you should never be content with JUST existing...start living!

You should never be content with just living a mediocre life. When one is content with simply existing, it usually results in a decrease of hunger and thirst for the better things that God has in store for their life. This does not mean that you will have access to all of the material possessions in the world. It means that you are working effectively to carry out your life's purpose and share His (God's) goodness with the world. Remember, your life is a testimony.

Truth is...you should never be happy in a stagnant condition.

Stagnation NEVER promotes growth! Seek to grow financially, spiritually and mentally in every area of your life. The time is N.O.W- New Opportunities Waiting.

101 Truths

Truth #46

Truth is...you are more than your appearance.

Your appearance is what is on the outside. People often judge others based on appearance; disregard those people who do this, because they do not appreciate the goodness that lies within you. However, do not deliberately try to deceive people by appearing as something you are not!

101 Truths

Truth is...beauty lies within.

Genuine beauty is not measured by outward appearance; instead, it is a measured by the contents of your spirit and soul. This is what God sees, and that is why He loves you so much!

Truth #48

Truth is...the only person you can control in life is yourself.

You cannot control what people say about you, how they look at you, or even how they perceive your actions. Do not worry about things you cannot control; instead, look to yourself and make sure you're doing what He requires of you.

Truth is...you need someone to help you in life.

No man is an island; everyone should have at least one person who they look up to, admire and trust. This person is an unconditional friend; they will promote your success and diminish your failures. Allow this person to help and guide you through life. Remember, you are never alone!

Truth is...you have the power to reverse the curse.

Pray diligently to break down strongholds. Pray without ceasing and believe the curses, if there are any, will be lifted. Vow to never speak a curse against anyone. Remember the rule…whatever you do to others always comes back to you.

101 Truths

Truth #51

Truth is...no one is better than you.

Do NOT compare yourself with another person. You are unique and you are capable of being as great as or even greater than the next person.

101 Truths

Truthful References

Isaiah 40:28-31 (NIV)
Psalms 33:4-6 (NIV)
Galatians 3:6-9 (NIV)
Psalms 112:1 (NIV)
Luke 12: 8-10 (NIV)
Romans 1:18-20 (NIV)
Nehemiah 8:10 (NIV)
1 Chronicles 16:11 (NIV)
Exodus 15:2 (NIV)
Jeremiah 17:5 (NIV)
Isaiah 41:10 (NIV)
Psalms 27:1 (NIV)
Romans 8:15 (NIV)
Isaiah 41:13 (NIV)
Psalms 23 (NIV)
1 Corinthians 16:13 (NIV)
Psalms 115:11 (NIV)
Matthew 10:28 (NIV)
Hebrews 13:5-6 (NIV)

Truths

About Your Life

Truth is...your life is a testimony!

When you "hold your tongue" (keep quiet), no one will know what God has done! Your testimony can help an individual who's going through the tests of life.

Truth #53

Truth is...life will not be easy, but the end result will be amazing.

L.I.F.E. to me means "Living Intended for Eternity". When you're living with an intention for eternity, you'll be kind to those who wrong you; you have to love those who hate you, and you will undoubtedly face many trials and tests. However, your reward is heaven bound where there will be no sighing or frowns.

101 Truths

Truth #54

Truth is...life is about free will.

God has given us the right to choose. Our choices directly shape and impact our lives. Be careful with this gift of free will. Make wise choices.

101 Truths

Truth #55

Truth is...everything in life happens for a reason.

Everything has a purpose. Seek to find the purpose of your personal life events, and you will begin to gain a deeper understanding; nothing is a coincidence.

Truth is...life will always have its ups and downs.

Think of life as a roller coaster; it can go up, come down and even involve some whirls. You can either enjoy the ride or try to hide. Learn from life's experiences; each moment has a lesson in store; seek to identify that lesson and LIVE!

Truth is...life is about helping people.

Jesus had a congregation of only 12 people; each of those individuals reached multitudes. You too are given the task of helping someone else. The Bible states, "what you have done for the least of these you have done it to me." (Matthew 25:40 NIV) Do good while you can!

Truth is...writing helps to keep your life in focus.

Jot down your goals and dreams. When you write things down on paper, you're producing a tangible product of which to hold onto. It allows you to put things into perspective, giving you a sense of accountability to yourself.

101 Truths

Truth #59

Truth is...you are responsible for the way you treat others.

Remember, adults are expected to take responsibility for their actions, so treat people accordingly. What you do to others will come back to you and your generation to follow. Your actions are the birthing of generational blessings and curses!

101 Truths

Truth #60

Truth...is your kindness will be repaid with evil SOMETIMES.

Although this is the case at times, you should not stop helping others. After all, they crucified Jesus, and yet He was blameless!

101 Truths

Truth #61

Truth is...evil will continue to seem as if it prospers.

There is only one judge and He is keeping record of all things. Continue to do well, and your reward will be found.

101 Truths

Truth #62

Truth is...hell was not prepared for you.

Hell was created for Satan (the Devil) and the fallen angles. However, they'd love it if you'd fall with them too. Be mindful of the decisions you make and the consequences that follow. Hell is real, and it is YOU who makes the ultimate decision concerning which door you will enter.

101 Truths

Truthful References

John 14:27 (NIV)
Psalms 46:1-3 (NIV)
John 16:33 (NIV)
Psalms 16:8 (NIV)
Psalms 119:25(NIV)
Psalms 120:1 (NIV)
2 Timothy 1:7 (NIV)
Proverbs 18:10 (NIV)
Psalms 55:22 (NIV)
Psalms 119:71 (NIV)
Psalms 119:50 (NIV)
Hebrews 11:1 (NIV)

Truths

About People, Family and Friends

Truth is...there are people who want nothing but your destruction.

There are people in this world that will appear to you like a "snake in the garden". They will deceive you into doing things, saying things, or acting in such a way that causes your destruction. Beware of people who encourage you to do wrong.

101 Truths

Truth #64

Truth is...people are always watching.

As mentioned, our lives are like television sets...always on display. What exactly does your life say?

101 Truths

Truth #65

Truth is...people can see your genuineness.

Be yourself, love who you are and be good at what you do. When you try to be something other than what you are, it is evident to others that you may not be genuine at all.

Truth is...people will sometimes hate you for no reason.

You do not have to offend a person for them to hate you; some people just see something great in you, and sometimes they'll feel threatened by what they see. Love them anyway!

Truth is...you are required to love and honor your parents.

There are some who have parents, yet they dislike them. Then, there are others who may not know their parents, but long to have a relationship with them. Regardless of your circumstance, know that the commandant is still true: "Honor your mother and father....." (Ephesians 6:2 NIV)

Truth is...family should be cherished.

Some people do not have a family to love, so cherish those you have; you may not like everything they do, but just know that family is a blessing and should not be taken for granted.

Truth is...generational curses are real.

As your family grows, you may observe various traits in your siblings or loved ones that you despise. Before you begin to condemn and judge, examine yourself to see where you may be at fault. Generational curses are passed down through one's particular bloodline throughout ongoing generations. Some of these curses are alcoholism, physical abuse, sexual abuse, emotional abuse and many other negative traits. These can only be broken through constant prayer and supplication.

Truth is...if money could buy your friends, then they wouldn't be good friends.

Learn to decipher who is for you and who is against you. If someone tries to put a "price" on you, let them know you cannot be bought. If that monetary figure impresses you, then you have devalued yourself. You are priceless....
a true treasure.

Truth #71

Truth is...it is easier to love someone than to like someone.

God requires that we love everyone and do well. However, liking people is another notion. There are various things you may dislike about someone. You may not like the way I write or who I am, but you should love the fact that I am trying to do the best I can do.

Truth is...conditional friendships should not exist.

Friendship is something I value greatly. Having friendships with "terms" attached should not exist. Also, if there are conditions that apply to your friendships, or if your friendships are based on mere feelings, it is not destined to last. Feelings are variable in nature....they change. Friendships should be constant and unchanging. Examine the "friends" in your circle; are they only around from time to time?

Truth is...people may see in you what you do not see in yourself.

The abilities and talents you possess are on display. Oftentimes, you need another person to help expose those abilities and passions you possess.What have others labeled as your area of expertise? These are things you do effortlessly and bring you joy. List 5 things that people have said you excel in and from that list choose the one you agree with most. With this one chosen channel your inner being and excel in this area.

Truth #74

Truth is...the "grass may be greener", but the water bill is higher!

The lives others live may appear to be more exciting or fun filled; even still, you do not know what they have done or endured to get to where they are today. Never covet (want/desire) what someone else has; work hard for what you want and appreciate what you have!

Truth is...if you can't beat em', don't join em'!

Too often, people are willing to conform to the "norm". This should not be; you have to be secure enough to stand alone, knowing that He (God) will always be with you. We need more leaders in the world; will you accept the leadership call?

101 Truths

Truthful References

Proverbs 22:24-25 (NIV)
Matthew 17:20 (NIV)
1 Peter 1:7 (NIV)
Proverbs 17:17 (NIV)
Titus 1:2 (NIV)
1 Peter 5:9 (NIV)
Proverbs 18:24 (NIV)
1 Corinthians 2:5 (NIV)
Psalms 103:17 (NIV)
2 Timothy 4:7 (NIV)
Ephesians 6:16 (NIV)
Ecclesiastes 4:9-10 (NIV)
Proverbs 12:26 (NIV)
John 15:12-15 (NIV)
Proverbs 13:20 (NIV)
Deuteronomy 5:16 (NIV)
Matthew 15:4 (NIV)
Proverbs 15:27 (NIV)

Truths

About Life, Love and God's Promises For You

101 Truths

Truth #76

Truth is....life is a journey.

Life can be an adventure; you will encounter many detours along the way. Just be patient and do not give in!

Truth is...life is not fair.

Life is not fair and it never will be. Even still, you should still do and become what He (God) requires of you.

101 Truths

Truth #78

Truth is...the words "love", "live", and "laugh" are all verbs.

We are taught in primary school that a verb is an action word. Therefore, loving, living and laughing are actions that should be practiced as long as you have life! Let's get moving!

Truth is...vengeance brings destruction.

When you seek to get revenge against someone who has wronged you, the only person who'll be left hurting is you. Learn to let go and leave things in God's hands.

Truth #80

Truth is...animosity/jealousy is a "disease", and it should not be present in your life.

If you are holding on to animosity/jealousy against another person, this "disease" you are carrying around is slowly killing you. Harboring hatred and animosity can act as a poison to your body. Just know that forgiveness is the cure, and there's no need for jealousy. Love YOU!

Truth is...God speaks in mysterious ways

God may not always speak directly to you; instead, He'll use people and situations to speak to you at times. Pray that your ears remain open to hear when He speaks, and that you'll grow in the ability to discern what He is trying to say.

101 Truths

Truth #82

Truth is...prayer is like water to the plant; it gives life.

Water is essential in life, because without it we could die. Your prayer life is like this water. You will not die a physical death, but you could die spiritually. Revive your spirit and soul with daily doses of prayer.

101 Truths

Truth #83

Truth is...words are seeds...be careful what you plant.

If you planted a grapefruit tree, would you expect oranges to grow? The same applies to your life. If all you continue to plant are seeds of "I can't, I hate, why can't I be like ____, I'm lazy, etc," what "fruits" do you expect to produce? You will only produce those negative "fruits" with these types of seeds planted. Your words are conditioning your actions. Learn to monitor what is planted in your life. Filter what you do and say; plant seeds of love today.

101 Truths

Truth #84

Truth is..."can't" should not be in your vocabulary.

The word "can't" can restrict, bind and halt all endeavors sought.
Remove it immediately; it is a hindrance in your life!

Truth #85

Truth is...loving material things more than we love Him is a ticket to hell.

When you idolize possessions and people more than God, He will not be pleased. Remember the Ten Commandments and seek to honor them.

101 Truths

Truth #86

Truth is...God can lift you up from your lowest point.

In times when you feel like you cannot go any further, remember the 'Footprints' story. Remember that when you do not have the strength to stand/walk, He will lift you up and carry you through. That is what the Father (God) can do!

101 Truths

Truth #87

Truth is...love is beautiful when it is pure.

God amazes me! He knows the most about us, yet His love for us still remains. Seek to love as purely as God does. Do not look at the other person's past; instead, love them for what they can be!

Truth is...there is only one true meteorologist, and He is God.

In the past couple of years, there have been unexplainable events occurring around the world. Some may link the events to Global Warming but I like to refer to it as God's Warning! When trying to understand the strange weather patterns, consult the "Book of Life".

Truth is...science cannot explain miracles.

Miracles happen every day, but we don't always hear about them. Share your miracle today. What has God done miraculous in your life this week, month or year?

101 Truths

Truth #90

Truth is...if you're going to name it, you should claim it.

Speak healing, speak joy, speak liberty, speak freedom, speak happiness and speak love over your life, claiming them all in Jesus' name.

101 Truths

Truth #91

Truth is...God is not finished with you yet.

There is so much more that God has in store for you. The situations that you may be facing are only shaping you and preparing you for greater things in life. Be patient and trust His will for your life.

101 Truths

Truth #92

Truth is...ALL children are blessings.

A child represents purity, truth, and the future. They bring joy and happiness to families and should be cherished. Bless them, do not curse them. Continue to pray for the children; pray that God guides them along the way. There are so many negative influences targeted at our youth, giving us the opportunity to be that positive role model today!

Truth is...a child should be raised to fear the Lord.

As a parent or guardian, you are the force that can establish a child's faith and allow them grow up to reverence and fear the Lord. Let us be mindful to cause our actions to positively reflect what we are saying to our children. If you are serving two masters (God and the Devil), it is likely that your children will too. You can be the force that pushes them to God, or away from Him.

Truth is...positive conditioning is so effective.

Conditioning is a powerful tool. I challenge you to condition your thinking to that of positive thoughts. In addition, condition your speech, remembering that words have power and the more you speak life, the greater you will become.

Truth is...when you fix your eyes on Him (God), He will guide you to higher heights.

This truth goes back to reiterate the first truth. God is the source of life through Jesus Christ, and Jesus Christ is the only way. He is everything! Getting lost in Him, and developing a newfound love and relationship with Him, will open endless opportunities.

101 Truths

Truth #96

Truth is...wisdom is worth far more than any amount of money in the world; thus, it cannot be bought.

Wisdom is one of the greatest gifts that can be attained. You can gain wisdom through prayer and supplication. Learn from others and make wise decisions. Wisdom is the engine that drives the vehicle of life.

Truth is...never share (with others) ALL of your plans and dreams.

Be mindful of what you share with others, because some only wish for your destruction. Keep a journal and talk to God. He will help direct, shape and equip you with skills needed to attain those goals and dreams, as long as they align with your destiny.

101 Truths

Truth #98

Truth is...love will not lie.

If you ever have to wonder whether or not it is love, please realize that true love will be transparent. Usually when you have to question whether or not it is love, the doubts you have may be very accurate. That "feel good" type of love is an illusion. What will happen when those feelings are gone? Be patient, and true love will come!

Truth is...I love you and God does too!

God's love is the greatest love of all! If you have not done so already, ask Him into your heart. God's plans for you are greater than any dreams. When you feel alone, rest assured that He has your best interest in store. He wants more for you than you may want for yourself. Seek Jesus Christ, accept the love He gives and seek to grow and glow in Him more and more!

Accepting Him is simple, repeat these words:
Dear Lord, I ask that you forgive me and cleanse me from all impurity. Help me to accept your love and live life pleasing to you. Guard my mind, eyes, ears and tongue that I may think, see, hear and speak things that will give you glory. Let my life be made whole and help me to sin no more.
In Jesus name I pray, Amen!

101 Truths

Truth #100

Truth is...He (God) promised NEVER to leave us nor forsake us. (Deuteronomy 31:6 NIV)

Whenever you feel alone, remember His promise and hold on! God is always around. Remember He (God) is Jehovah Jireh (your provider). He is your comfort when you need it most; He acts as your feet when you cannot walk; He reads your tears when your words cannot be formed; He lifts you up when you have fallen down. God can and will provide anything you need according to His riches in Christ Jesus. He reads the heart and He knows what we need before we even ask. Call on Him and He will ALWAYS be there! Seek Him and He will always be found.

Truth is...you were born into sin, but you are destined to win!

This last truth is also of great importance. Since the beginning of time, we were all born into sin after the deception took place (see Genesis Chapter 3 NIV). Although we are born into sin, we are destined to win. Life is a race; not for the swift or strong, but for all of those who endure it all along. It does not matter how long it takes; run the race, finish first place and succeed! God's plans for your life exceed your own. Remember, the only competition is you! Are you ready to stop holding yourself back?

101 Truths

Truthful References

Romans 8:38-39 (NIV)
Job 6:8 (NIV)
Proverbs 13:12 (NIV)
Job 11:18-19 (NIV)
Psalms 147:11 (NIV)
Romans 3:23 (NIV)
Hebrews 7:25 (NIV)
Proverbs 14:27 (NIV)
Proverbs 18:21 (NIV)
1 Timothy 6:12 (NIV)
1 John 5:20 (NIV)
John 14:6 (NIV)
Ephesians 2:4 (NIV)
Hebrews 4:16 (NIV)
John 11:25-26 (NIV)
Romans 6:23 (NIV)
Luke 6:36 (NIV)

101 Truths

Truth #102

MY LIFELONG TRUTH

In the space below, create your truth. Write it and make it
clear and seek to remember this truth every day.

_____

_____

_____

_____

_____

Acknowledgements

Oswald Thomas- Daddy, you are a hard working individual who possesses many skills and abilities. Does anyone need a plumber, electrician, carpenter, builder or musician? You name it, my dad, the "jack of all trades", can do it! Thank you for believing in me and encouraging me to DO better and BE better. I love you and will continue to strive to make you proud. I'll forever be daddy's little girl.

Rev. Lynette Thomas- You are my mother, my rock, best friend and best Caribbean cook of ALL! You have the biggest heart and would give the very clothes off your back if someone needed them. No one ever remains hungry in your presence; for you supply the most amazing food ever! I aspire to be half the woman you are; a woman of great integrity and loyalty. I love you with every breath I take, and will continue to strive to make you proud! I'm so blessed to have you around! Please visit www.brooklynemmanuel-wesleyan.org for church updates.

McKinley Thomas- My brother, the BEST gentleman in the WORLD! It has always been just us two. We fight, laugh and cry together, and I love you for who you are! Nothing or no one can break our bond. You truly are anointed, and I encourage you to continue to pursue all of your goals and dreams. God has so much more in store for you and I cannot wait to celebrate with you. Thank you for always encouraging me and for always believing in me...even when I did not believe in myself. I will forever love you, your little sister!

Rev. Hansely Griffith- As my adopted/spiritual "father" and guide, you encouraged me to pursue my goals and dreams, and to you I am forever grateful. Thank you for your continued prayers and support. You are truly a dynamic man of God; continue to do His Kingdom work! Rev. Hansely Griffith is founder and CEO of Family Heartbeat International Network. Visit http://familyheartbeat.org for more information.

Icia Ragsdale- You helped me to align my purpose for writing and have instructed me on ways to accomplish my goal. When I met you in April of 2012, which was definitely a divine connection, you signed something in your book for me that resonates with me today. Thank you for who you are and what you are doing! Icia Ragsdale is the author of "Letters 4 You"; a testimonial of God's love and His faithfulness to set His people free. Please visit http://iciaragsdale.com/ to support her efforts by purchasing her book.

To my "adopted" family and friends, I love each of you dearly! Antonette W., Ruth D., Micki G., Hazel and Syndey D., Joyce J., Connie L., Alverda M., Joanne J., Tiffany D., Crystal G., Natalee S., Sharron R., Nyasha T., Lorella J., Mike and Esther B., Lauren B., Lovanda C., and Monokia N.... you all are AWESOME, and I am blessed to have met each of you! Thank you for being who you are in my life! To my numerous family members and other friends—including aunts, uncles, cousins, in-laws—who are in Guyana, Barbados, Holland, Curacao, New York, Ohio, Canada, Maryland and everywhere else, thank you for every kind word, and even truthful (sometimes hurtful) remarks that you have spoken. You all have assisted in shaping my life. I am forever grateful to all of you! Thank you, thank you, and thank you again!

CPSIA information can be obtained at www.ICGtesting.com
Printed in the USA
BVOW080259200613

323705BV00002B/5/P

9 780615 810348